CHOCOLATE ASTROLOGY

Delectable Recipes and Readings for Every Sign of the Zodiac

CHOCOLATE ASTROLOGY

With text and illusrations by Joy Nagy

Clarkson Potter/Publishers   New York

Published by Clarkson Potter/Publishers, New York, New York.
Member of the Crown Publishing Group, a division of Random House, Inc.
www.randomhouse.com

CLARKSON N. POTTER is a trademark and POTTER
and colophon are registered trademarks of Random House, Inc.

Recipes created for "Sagittarius," "Libra," "Taurus," "Virgo," "Aquarius,"
"Cancer," "Pisces," and "Gemini" desserts and all chocolate confections
were created by Jean Galton.

Printed in Singapore

Design by Caitlin Daniels Israel
Illustrations by Joy Nagy

Library of Congress Cataloging-in-Publication Data is available upon request.

ISBN 0-609-60941-6

10 9 8 7 6 5 4 3 2 1

First Edition

CONTENTS

INTRODUCTION

Milk chocolate, bittersweet chocolate, dark chocolate, white chocolate. Cakes, cookies, brownies, candies, truffles, puddings, and drinks. Sometimes it seems there are as many different forms and varieties of chocolate as there are stars in the sky.

Are you a milk chocolate fan, a dark chocolate devotee, a bittersweet chocolate aficionado, or a white chocolate lover? Perhaps the answer is tied to your birth sign! For centuries, people have looked to the movement of the stars and the planets to learn more about their personalities and what the world holds in store for them. Chocolate, as well, has historically been believed to have mystical powers of its own. Popularly considered an aphrodisiac, it has helped many a lover woo and seduce. After all, what Valentine's Day would be complete without a heart-shaped box of chocolate delights?

But chocolate has had wondrous charms for much longer than there have been shiny red boxes. When Spanish explorers arrived in Central America in the seventeenth century, they were introduced to a sacred Aztec beverage called *xocolatl*, made from the cocoa bean. The Aztecs believed the drink possessed extraordinary powers to impart wisdom, strength, and sensuality. When the Spanish explorers brought their discovery back to Europe, it first was touted as a medicine, then was enjoyed as a luxury drink by the aristocracy, and finally was popularized by the masses. For hundreds of years, chocolate's mysterious magnetism has continued to entice and enchant people the world over.

Chocolate Astrology combines the power of the planets and the power of this most alluring of treats. What is your chocolate personality? Do you stash chocolates in your desk drawer, or do you travel to the ends of the earth in search of exotic new tastes? Do you prefer the rich, deep taste of dark chocolate or the silky texture of the smoothest milk chocolate? Look inside to find out how your birth sign, your personality, and your chocolate preferences intersect in unusual, unexpected ways. Then try the astrologically inspired recipes and discover for yourself the charms of your sign's special chocolate!

 "Chocolate is not only pleasant of taste, but it's also a veritable balm of the mouth, for the maintaining of all glands and humors in a good state of health. Thus it is, that all who drink it possess a sweet breath."
—Italian physician Stephani Blancardi (1650–1702)

Aries, Leo, and Sagittarius

THEIR BIRTH CHOCOLATE: BITTERSWEET CHOCOLATE

Bittersweet chocolate is the richest and darkest of chocolates because it has the highest ratio of pure cocoa extract to sugar and cocoa butter. People born under the fire signs delight in the strong flavor of bittersweet chocolate, and the taste often sparks passionate feelings in them.

Aries, Leo, and Sagittarius are known for their strength, leadership, and assertiveness. The tangy intensity of bittersweet chocolate is the perfect complement to these fiery personalities.

Hardworking and focused, Aries is satisfied by the rewards of a job well done. Whether building monuments or a financial portfolio, this sign rises to a challenge and can almost always be assured of success.

Dramatic and proud, Leo wears a crown while doling out an array of splendid food. Ruled by the imperial Sun, the Lion will not yield until his request for chocolate is fulfilled.

There's nothing more compelling to a Sagittarius than an airplane ticket. Any time, any place, the Archer leaps at the chance for a travel adventure, provided he or she doesn't have other commitments. If it's possible, however, you can be sure Sagittarius will figure out a way to enjoy both events.

Fire Sign

ARIES

THE RAM
March 21–April 19

BITTERSWEET CHOCOLATE–COVERED CHERRIES

The bittersweet chocolate coating honors Mars, Aries's fiery planetary ruler. Inside, a sweet cherry symbolizes the fresh beginnings of spring, the sign's birth season.

The Ram is an impulsive leader, full of energy and self-confidence. The spontaneous, romantic people born under this sign enjoy picnicking or sipping champagne beneath a starry sky—always with a box of chocolates close at hand.

Aries Bittersweet Chocolate–Covered Cherries

makes 24

2 cups red wine

1 cup sugar

2 strips (1 × 2 inches each) lemon zest

2 dozen ripe cherries with stems, pitted

6 ounces bittersweet chocolate, melted

1 ounce white chocolate, chopped, optional

The artist Beatrice Wood, who died in 1999, attributed her longevity of 105 years to "chocolate and young men."

1. Combine the wine, sugar, and zest in a small heavy saucepan. Bring to a boil. Add the cherries and simmer for 2 minutes. Remove from the heat and let the cherries cool in the pan. Remove the cherries from the saucepan and drain thoroughly.

2. Holding each cherry by its stem, dip into the melted bittersweet chocolate. Place on a baking sheet lined with parchment or wax paper. Refrigerate until set, about 20 minutes.

3. Place the white chocolate in a glass measuring cup or bowl and microwave on medium for 30 seconds. Stir and microwave for 10 to 30 seconds longer, or until melted. Scrape the chocolate into a small plastic sandwich bag. Snip off a small piece of a bottom corner and pipe the Aries sign onto each cherry. Refrigerate until set. Keep the cherries refrigerated until time to serve (they will keep for 2 days).

Aries Chocolate Cake with Bittersweet Chocolate Glaze

serves 8

CAKE

2 cups sifted cake flour

1 teaspoon baking soda

$^1/_2$ teaspoon salt

$^1/_2$ cup (1 stick) unsalted butter, at room temperature

$1^1/_2$ cups sugar

3 large eggs, separated

2 teaspoons vanilla extract

3 ounces (3 squares) unsweetened chocolate, melted and cooled

1 cup sour cream

GLAZE

$^1/_2$ cup heavy cream

3 ounces bittersweet chocolate, coarsely chopped

1 tablespoon dark rum

1. Preheat the oven to 350°F. Grease two 9-inch round cake pans. Line the bottoms with parchment or wax paper. Grease the parchment and dust the pans with flour; tap out the excess.

2. In a medium bowl, combine the flour, soda, and salt. Mix well and set aside.

3. In a large bowl, beat the butter with an electric mixer on medium-high speed until smooth and creamy. Gradually add the sugar, then continue beating until the butter mixture has increased in volume and is very light and fluffy, about 8 minutes. Add the egg yolks, one at a time, beating well after each addition. Beat in the vanilla and the chocolate.

4. With the mixer on low, alternately add the flour mixture and the sour cream to the batter, beginning and ending with the flour and beating just until blended.

5. In another clean bowl, beat the egg whites with an electric mixer (with clean beaters) at medium speed until the peaks are stiff but not dry. With a rubber spatula, fold a third of the whites into the batter until well mixed. Gently fold in the remaining whites just until blended. Divide the batter between the prepared pans and bake about 25 minutes, or just until a cake tester inserted comes out clean. Let cool for 15 minutes in the pans, then invert onto racks to cool completely.

6. To make the glaze, bring the cream to a boil in a small saucepan. Remove from the heat, add the chocolate, and whisk until smooth. Stir in the rum. With a spatula, spread two-thirds of the glaze over the tops of both cake layers. Arrange one layer on top of the other and drizzle the remaining glaze over the sides.

LEO

THE LION
July 23–August 22

BITTERSWEET CHOCOLATE LEMON CUPS

The regal soul of the Leo appreciates the rich luxury of bittersweet chocolate, and the tangy lemon filling pleases this sign's sunny heart and outgoing spirit. A true Leo, warmhearted and magnanimous, seeks a partner to share this delectable experience.

Leo Bittersweet Chocolate Lemon Cups

makes 50

$1^1/_4$ pounds tempered bittersweet chocolate
(see How to Temper Chocolate, page 90)

Confectioners' sugar

2 teaspoons finely grated lemon zest

$^1/_4$ teaspoon pure lemon oil

Basic Fondant Filling (see page 92)

2 ounces white chocolate, chopped, optional

"What cartridges in battle? I always
carry chocolate instead."

—The Chocolate Soldier,
in G. B. Shaw's *Arms and the Man*

1. With a small paintbrush, coat the insides of 50 small (confection-size) paper candy cups with the tempered chocolate. Refrigerate until firm. Coat once more with the chocolate and refrigerate until firm.

2. On a work surface dusted with confectioners' sugar, knead the lemon zest and oil into the fondant until thoroughly incorporated. Roll into a $1/2$-inch-wide cylinder and cut into $1/2$-inch pieces.

3. Place a piece of fondant in each cup and spoon melted chocolate over the fondant, sealing it thoroughly. Fill each cup with the chocolate until level and full. Refrigerate until set.

4. Place the white chocolate in a glass measuring cup or bowl and microwave on medium for 30 to 40 seconds. Stir and microwave for 10 to 40 seconds longer, or until melted. Scrape the chocolate into a small plastic sandwich bag. Snip off a small piece of a bottom corner and pipe the Leo sign onto each cup. Refrigerate until set, peel off the wrappers, and place the cups in clean foil candy cups.

Leo Bittersweet
Chocolate Cupcakes

makes 12

CUPCAKES

1 cup all-purpose flour

1 teaspoon baking soda

$^1/_4$ teaspoon salt

4 tablespoons ($^1/_2$ stick) unsalted butter, at room temperature

1 cup packed dark brown sugar

1 large egg, at room temperature

1 teaspoon vanilla extract

$1^1/_2$ ounces ($1^1/_2$ squares) unsweetened chocolate, melted and cooled

$^1/_2$ cup sour cream, at room temperature

$^1/_2$ cup boiling water

ICING

3 ounces (3 squares) unsweetened chocolate

3 tablespoons unsalted butter, cut up

$2^{1}/_{4}$ cups sifted confectioners' sugar

1 teaspoon vanilla extract

$^{1}/_{3}$ cup sour cream

1. Preheat the oven to 350°F. Line twelve $2^{1}/_{2}$- or 3-inch muffin cups with paper cupcake liners. In a medium bowl, stir together the flour, baking soda, and salt.

2. In a large bowl, beat the butter and brown sugar with an electric mixer on medium-high speed until smooth and creamy. Beat in the egg, then the vanilla, and finally the chocolate.

3. With mixer on low, alternately add the flour mixture and the sour cream to the batter, beginning and ending with the flour and beating just until blended. Beat in the boiling water. Pour the mixture into the prepared muffin tins and bake for 20 minutes, or just until a cake tester inserted comes out clean. Let cool completely on racks.

4. To make the icing, combine the chocolate and butter in a glass measuring cup or bowl. Microwave on medium for 1 to 2 minutes, stirring a few times, or until the butter is melted and the mixture is smooth. Transfer to a large bowl or the bowl of an electric mixer.

5. Beat in $1^{1}/_{2}$ cups of the confectioners' sugar and the vanilla with an electric mixer on medium speed. Beat in the sour cream, then the remaining sugar, until the icing is smooth, about 1 minute. Ice the cupcakes and serve.

Fire Sign

SAGITTARIUS

THE ARCHER
November 22–December 21

BITTERSWEET CHOCOLATES
WITH GINGER CREAM FILLING

The exotic Asian-influenced taste of this ginger cream confection draws the travel-loving Sagittarius, and the bittersweet chocolate coating adds just the right contrast. Sagittarius, the Archer, is a swashbuckling, courageous, athletic optimist. Expect this sign to explore all the distant corners of the earth in search of unusual new chocolate tastes.

Sagittarius Bittersweet Chocolates with Ginger Cream Filling

makes about 25

Confectioners' sugar

$1/4$ cup finely chopped crystallized ginger

Basic Fondant Filling (see page 92)

$1^1/4$ pound tempered bittersweet chocolate
(see How to Temper Chocolate, page 90)

1 ounce white chocolate, chopped, optional

"Of all the foods on earth, it may be true that
a craving for chocolate is the most universal."
—Craig Claiborne,
New York Times food writer

1. On a work surface liberally dusted with confectioners' sugar, knead the ginger into the fondant until evenly distributed. Roll into a 3/4-inch cylinder and cut into 1/2-inch pieces. Roll each piece into a ball and flatten slightly with the palm of your hand.

2. With a fork or candy-dipper, dip each piece of fondant into the tempered chocolate. Place on a cookie sheet lined with parchment or wax paper. Refrigerate until the chocolate is firm.

3. Place the white chocolate in a glass measuring cup or bowl and microwave on medium for 30 seconds. Stir and microwave for 10 to 30 seconds longer, or until melted. Scrape the chocolate into a small plastic sandwich bag. Snip off a small piece of a bottom corner and pipe the Sagittarius sign on each chocolate.

Sagittarius Chocolate Hazelnut Cookies

makes about 38

2 cups hazelnuts

1 $^{1}/_{2}$ cups sugar

12 ounces almond paste

$^{1}/_{4}$ cup unsweetened cocoa powder, preferably Dutch process

Pinch of salt

4 large egg whites, at room temperature

1. Preheat the oven to 350°F. Spread the hazelnuts on a cookie sheet and bake until the skins are blackened and the nuts are lightly browned, about 15 minutes. Transfer the warm nuts to a kitchen towel and rub briskly to remove the skins. Coarsely chop 1/2 cup of the nuts and set aside.

2. Combine the remaining hazelnuts with the sugar in a food processor fitted with a steel blade, and grind to a fine powder. Add the almond paste and process until well mixed. Add the cocoa and salt and process until mixed, scraping down the bowl several times.

3. With the motor running, pour the egg whites and chopped hazelnuts into the hazelnut mixture. Process just until mixed.

4. Spoon heaping tablespoonfuls of the batter 1 1/2 inches apart onto parchment-lined baking sheets. Bake for 18 to 20 minutes, or until the cookies are firm on the outside but still chewy inside. Let them cool for 5 minutes on the baking sheet and then transfer to a rack to cool completely.

THE EARTH SIGNS:

Taurus, Virgo, and Capricorn

THEIR BIRTH CHOCOLATE: DARK CHOCOLATE

Unlike other chocolates, dark chocolate is best when it stands on its own, making it particularly suitable for the solid, independent earth signs. Sensual and earthy, Tauruses, Virgos, and Capricorns appreciate the depth and full-bodied flavor of the best dark chocolates. These signs enjoy the entire aesthetic experience of eating a rich piece of dark chocolate, including taste, texture, appearance, and smell.

Solid and strong, Taurus enjoys basking in the outdoors. An inveterate hedonist, the bull makes any excuse to enjoy the abundant pleasures of nature.

Virgos can spend hours fussing over details and creating the perfect home. In service to others, a Virgo is always ready to work for a worthy cause.

A Capricorn will go to any lengths to gain the most beautiful and expensive object the universe offers. Every stairway leads the Goat to potential success.

TAURUS

THE BULL
April 20–May 20

Dark Chocolate Truffles
with Chestnut Cream Filling

The sumptuous combination of rich dark chocolate paired with smooth chestnut cream appeals to Taurus, a sensual lover of nature and luxury.

Taurus, the Bull, is dependable and loyal. Taureans are known for their high standards, and they never compromise when selecting the finest chocolate.

Taurus Dark Chocolate Truffles with Chestnut Cream Filling

makes 48

24 ounces semisweet chocolate, finely chopped

¹/₂ cup canned chestnut puree

¹/₃ cup heavy cream

1 tablespoon brandy or Cognac

1 ounce white chocolate, finely chopped, optional

"The Spanish ladies of the New World are madly addicted to chocolate to such a point that they are not content to drink it several times each day, they have it served to them in church."

—ANTHELME BRILLAT-SAVARIN COOKBOOK AUTHOR, 1755–1826

1. Place 8 ounces of the semisweet chocolate and the chestnut puree in the bowl of a food processor. Bring the cream to a boil in a small saucepan and, with the processor's motor running, pour the cream into the chocolate mixture. Process until smooth, then pour in the Cognac with the motor running. Process until well mixed and, with a spatula, scrape into a mixing bowl. Refrigerate until thick and stiff, about 3 to 4 hours.

2. Chill a baking sheet and line it with wax or parchment paper. Use a melon baller to shape the chocolate into 3/4-inch balls on the baking sheet. Cover with plastic wrap and freeze until chilled, about 1 to 2 hours.

3. Temper (see How to Temper Chocolate, page 90) the remaining semisweet chocolate and, using a fork or candy-dipper, dip the chocolates into it one at a time. Place them on a baking sheet lined with parchment or wax paper and let stand until set.

4. To decorate, place the white chocolate in a glass measuring cup or bowl and microwave on medium for 30 seconds. Stir and microwave for 10 to 30 seconds longer, or until melted. Scrape the chocolate into a small plastic sandwich bag. Snip off a small piece of a bottom corner and pipe the Taurus sign onto each truffle. Refrigerate until set.

Taurus Chocolate Eclair

makes 8 eclairs

3/4 cup water

6 tablespoons (3/4 stick) unsalted butter

1/8 teaspoon salt

2 teaspoons plus 1 tablespoon sugar

3/4 cup all-purpose flour

4 large eggs

4 ounces semisweet chocolate, chopped

1 1/2 cups heavy cream

1 teaspoon vanilla extract

1. Preheat the oven to 400°F. Line two cookie sheets with parchment paper, or grease and flour them.

2. Combine the water, butter, salt, and 2 teaspoons of the sugar in a 2-quart saucepan. Bring to a boil. Stir until the butter has melted and the sugar has dissolved. Transfer the pot to a dishtowel placed on the counter. Add the flour and stir quickly with a wooden spoon until the mixture forms a ball (it will be lumpy at first; keep stirring until it becomes smooth).

3. Break one egg into the mixture and beat vigorously with a wooden spoon until the egg is completely blended into the mixture. Repeat with two more eggs (there will be one egg remaining).

4. Transfer the mixture to a pastry bag fitted with a 1-inch plain tip. Pipe 8 eclair shapes (each $4 \times 1^1/2$ inches wide) 2 inches apart on the cookie sheets. Alternately, spoon the eclair shapes onto the cookie sheets and smooth the tops with your finger dipped in water. Beat the remaining egg lightly with a teaspoon of water and lightly brush the eclairs with the egg. Bake for 20 minutes, then reduce the heat to 350°F. Bake until golden brown and very firm to the touch, about 20 to 25 minutes. Shut off the oven and poke the ends of each eclair with a skewer. Return to the oven for 10 minutes longer to dry the insides of the eclairs a bit. Transfer to a rack to cool. With a serrated knife, cut off the top third of each eclair. Remove any uncooked dough from the inside of the eclairs with your fingers.

5. To make the top glaze: place the chocolate in a mixing bowl. Bring $1/2$ cup of the cream to a boil and pour it over the chocolate. Whisk until smooth.

6. Dip the top of each eclair into the glaze and place, glaze side up, on a baking sheet to dry. Reserve the remaining glaze to use in the filling.

7. To make the filling: with an electric mixer, whip the remaining 1 cup of cream with the remaining 1 tablespoon of sugar and the vanilla. Fold the remaining glaze into the whipped cream and with a spoon or pastry bag, fill the bottoms of the eclairs with the chocolate whipped cream filling. Place the glazed tops over the filling and refrigerate until the tops are set, or until ready to serve.

VIRGO

THE VIRGIN
August 23–September 22

THE PERFECT CHOCOLATE FOR A VIRGO:
DARK CHOCOLATE TRUFFLES

The elegant dark chocolate truffle mirrors this sign's quiet sensuality and sweet simplicity. Most of all, it is the truffle's understated charm that attracts the cool, collected, intellectual Virgo.

Virgos are detail-oriented, dependable, and reliable. They will be the first to point out loose wrappers on a tray of chocolates, collect them, and proceed to arrange the remaining chocolates neatly.

Virgo Dark Chocolate Truffles

makes 35 to 40

24 ounces semisweet chocolate, finely chopped

¹/₂ cup heavy cream

2 tablespoons Cognac or brandy

1 ounce white chocolate, finely chopped, optional

"*Xocolatl* [chocolate] . . . storm in the blood
that comes in through the mouth . . ."
—FRIDA KAHLO, *The Diary of Frida Kahlo*

1. Place 8 ounces of the semisweet chocolate in a bowl. Bring the cream to a boil in a small saucepan and pour it over the chocolate. Whisk until smooth, then whisk in the Cognac. Refrigerate until thick and stiff, about 3 to 4 hours.

2. Chill a baking sheet and line it with wax or parchment paper. Using a melon baller or a pastry bag fitted with a $^1/_2$-inch plain tip, shape the chocolate into $^3/_4$-inch balls on the baking sheet. Cover with plastic wrap and refrigerate until chilled, about 2 to 3 hours.

3. Remove the chocolates from the refrigerator to warm up. Temper (see How to Temper Chocolate, page 90) the remaining semisweet chocolate and, using a fork or candy-dipper, dip the chocolates in one at a time. Place them on a baking sheet lined with parchment or wax paper. Let stand until set.

4. To decorate, place the white chocolate in a glass measuring cup or bowl and microwave on medium for 30 seconds. Stir and microwave for 10 to 30 seconds longer, or until melted. Scrape the chocolate into a small plastic sandwich bag. Snip off a small piece of a bottom corner and pipe the Virgo sign onto each truffle. Refrigerate until set.

Virgo Layer Cake

serves 6 to 8

3/4 cup sifted cake flour

1/4 cup cocoa, preferably Dutch process

1/2 teaspoon salt

6 large eggs, separated and at room temperature

1 cup granulated sugar

1 teaspoon vanilla extract

1 1/2 cups heavy cream

1/4 cup confectioners' sugar

4 teaspoons raspberry liqueur

1 1/2 cups fresh raspberries

1. Preheat the oven to 350°F. Grease a 17¹/₂ × 11¹/₂-inch jellyroll pan and line the bottom with wax paper or parchment.

2. Sift together the cake flour, cocoa, and salt and set aside.

3. In the bowl of an electric mixer, beat the egg yolks and ¹/₂ cup of the granulated sugar on high speed until pale and thick, about 3 minutes. Beat in the vanilla. With a spatula, fold in the flour mixture.

4. In another bowl, with the whisk attachment of the mixer, beat the egg whites on medium speed until frothy. Then beat on high speed, slowly adding the remaining ¹/₂ cup of sugar, and beat until the whites are stiff but not dry. With a spatula, fold a third of the whites into the yolk mixture. Then fold the remaining whites into the mixture, just until mixed. Pour into the prepared pan and smooth to the edges. Bake for 25 to 30 minutes, or until the top springs back when lightly touched. Let the cake cool in the pan for 5 minutes, then run a thin-bladed knife around the edge of the cake to loosen it from the sides. Press a cooling rack over the top of the pan and invert the cake onto the rack. Pull off the parchment and let the cake cool.

5. With a sharp serrated knife, cut the cake in half crosswise and in half lengthwise to form four pieces, about 9 × 6-inches each.

6. To make the filling, in a large bowl whip the cream with the confectioners' sugar and liqueur until stiff. Reserve ¹/₂ cup of the cream mixture. Spread a third of the remaining cream mixture (about a heaping ¹/₂ cup) over the first layer of cake. Top with another cake layer and spread another third of the cream over it. Top with another cake layer and the remaining cream. Cover with the remaining layer and tightly cover with plastic wrap. Refrigerate until chilled, at least 1 hour. To serve, cut into serving pieces and dollop with the remaining whipped cream. Top with fresh raspberries and serve.

Earth Sign

CAPRICORN

THE GOAT

December 22–January 19

FIVE SPICE CHOCOLATES

Capricorns are serious, conservative, and conscientious, and it takes a lot for them to show playfulness. Spiced dark chocolates are a dignified treat for this reserved sign.

Like the surefooted mountain climber that is its symbol, Capricorn the Goat always finds sweet success at the summit of every challenge. And although Capricorns may be workaholics, they often keep chocolate rewards stashed in their desk drawers!

Capricorn Five Spice Chocolates

makes about 34

$^1/_4$ teaspoon Five Spice powder (available in most supermarkets)

$1^1/_4$ pounds tempered semisweet chocolate
(see How to Temper Chocolate, page 90)

1 ounce white chocolate, finely chopped, optional

"The superiority of chocolate (hot chocolate), both for health and nourishment will soon give it the same preference over tea and coffee in America which it has in Spain." —THOMAS JEFFERSON

1. Mix the Five Spice powder into the dark chocolate until smooth. With a pastry bag and a small, plain tip, pipe the chocolate into candy molds (which can be purchased from confectionery manufacture suppliers or other specialty stores). Drop each mold (open side up) gently on the work surface to force out any bubbles. With a knife, scrape across the top of the mold to remove any excess chocolate. Refrigerate for 10 to 20 minutes, or until firm.

2. Invert the chocolates onto a piece of wax or parchment paper. To decorate the tops, place the white chocolate in a glass measuring cup or bowl and microwave on medium for 30 to 40 seconds. Stir and microwave for 10 to 40 seconds longer, or until melted. Scrape the chocolate into a small plastic sandwich bag. Snip off a small piece of a bottom corner and pipe the Capricorn sign onto each chocolate. Refrigerate until set.

Capricorn Chocolate Yeast Cake

serves 12

CAKE

2 (.25 ounce each) packets dry yeast

1 teaspoon plus $^1/_3$ cup sugar

$^1/_4$ cup warm water

4 cups all-purpose flour

$^1/_2$ teaspoon salt

4 ounces (1 stick) unsalted butter

1 cup warm milk

1 large egg plus 1 egg yolk

FILLING

1 cup unsweetened cocoa

1 cup sugar

2 ounces ($^1/_2$ stick) unsalted butter, cut into small bits

1. Combine the yeast, 1 teaspoon of sugar, and the water in a small bowl. Let stand for 10 to 15 minutes, or until the yeast has become creamy.

2. Meanwhile, sift the flour, $1/3$ cup sugar, and salt together into a large bowl. With your fingers, two knives, or a pastry cutter, rub in the butter until it forms small crumbs. In a small bowl, combine the milk, egg, yolk, and the yeast mixture. Pour into the flour and stir until a sticky ball comes together. Turn out onto a heavily floured surface and knead, adding extra flour as needed (this is a very sticky dough), for about 5 minutes, or until the dough is smooth and less sticky. Place the dough in a lightly buttered bowl and turn to coat it with butter. Cover with a clean dishcloth and set in a warm place for about 2 to 3 hours, or until the dough has doubled in size.

3. On a lightly floured surface, roll the dough into a 20 × 15-inch rectangle. To make the filling, mix together the cocoa and 1 cup of sugar in a small bowl and sprinkle over the dough. Dot with the butter. Roll the dough up along the short length, tucking the ends in as you go along (so the filling doesn't fall out), and place it seam side down in a buttered 10 × 4-inch angel food cake pan or ring pan. Cover with the cloth again and let rise in a warm place until the dough reaches the top of the pan, about $1^{1}/_{2}$ to 2 hours.

4. Preheat the oven to 350°F. and bake for 50 to 55 minutes, until nicely browned and the cake sounds hollow when tapped on the bottom. Let the cake cool on a rack and turn it out of the pan.

Cancer, Scorpio, and Pisces

THEIR BIRTH CHOCOLATE: MILK CHOCOLATE

Milk chocolate is fluid and smooth, offering a special emotional and psychic comfort to the water signs, who intuitively connect with this variety of chocolate above all others. Expect the water signs to feel a deep tie to this luxurious chocolate.

Milk chocolate's soft color and texture lull the water signs into a feeling of safety and familiarity. When times are stressful, Cancer, Scorpio, and Pisces find great comfort and security in a milk chocolate bar.

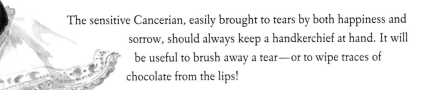

The sensitive Cancerian, easily brought to tears by both happiness and sorrow, should always keep a handkerchief at hand. It will be useful to brush away a tear—or to wipe traces of chocolate from the lips!

Scorpios always want to keep their secrets in a locked box, but outwardly their industriousness and resolve assure success in every personal or professional challenge.

Mystical Pisces, lover of life and spirituality, is represented by two fish, which symbolize the opposite choices available for any decision.

Water Sign

CANCER

THE CRAB
June 22–July 22

MILK CHOCOLATES WITH ORANGE CREAM FILLING

Cancer is one of the most sensitive and emotional of the signs, but sometimes this moonchild must hide a soft interior beneath a self-protective exterior. For that reason, soft fruit-flavored creams inside a hard milk chocolate coating particularly resonate with this sign.

Cancers are caring, emotional, family-oriented homebodies. They will spend hours shopping for the perfect box of chocolates for a special loved one.

Cancer Milk Chocolates with Orange Cream Filling

makes about 50

Confectioners' sugar

1 tablespoon grated orange zest

$^1/_4$ teaspoon orange flower water

Basic Fondant Filling (see page 92)

$2^1/_2$ pounds milk chocolate, tempered
(see How to Temper Chocolate, page 90)

2 ounces white chocolate, chopped, optional

"We understand each other, chocolate and I. My husband says I can hear chocolate." —MAIDA HEATTER, COOKBOOK AUTHOR

1. On a work surface liberally dusted with confectioners' sugar, knead the orange zest and orange flower water into the fondant. Roll into a 1/2-inch-wide cylinder and cut into 1/4-inch pieces.

2. Using a pastry bag, pipe the milk chocolate into candy molds (which can be purchased from candy and confectionery manufacture suppliers or other specialty stores). Drop each mold (open side up) gently onto the work surface to force out any bubbles. After 2 minutes, turn the mold upside down and shake out any excess chocolate onto a piece of wax paper, using a circular motion to coat the mold completely. With a knife, scrape across the top of the mold to remove any excess chocolate. Place the molds face down, so they thicken at their bases. Refrigerate for 10 to 20 minutes, or until firm.

3. Place a piece of fondant in each mold. Pipe in more tempered milk chocolate to cover the fondant. Scrape the top to level the chocolate and refrigerate until set, about 10 to 20 minutes. Invert the molds onto a sheet of wax paper.

4. To decorate the tops, place the white chocolate in a glass measuring cup or bowl and microwave on medium for 30 to 40 seconds. Stir, then microwave for 10 to 40 seconds longer, or until melted. Scrape the chocolate into a small plastic sandwich bag. Snip off a small piece of a bottom corner and pipe horizontal stripes and the Cancer sign onto each chocolate. Refrigerate until set.

Cancer Hot Chocolate

makes 4 cups

4 ounces milk chocolate, finely chopped

1 cup water

Pinch of salt

2 cups milk

1 cup heavy cream

1 teaspoon vanilla extract

In the top of a double boiler set over simmering
water, combine the chocolate, water, and salt. Stir
until the chocolate melts. Stir in the milk and cream and heat,
uncovered, until hot, stirring frequently. Stir in the vanilla
and serve.

 *In the eighteenth century, coffee symbolized
the rising middle classes while cocoa was the
drink of the aristocracy.*

Water Sign

SCORPIO

THE SCORPION
October 23– November 21

THE PERFECT CHOCOLATE FOR A SCORPIO:

Milk Chocolate Truffles with Rum Raisin Cream Filling

With its seductive flavor, rum raisin appeals to Scorpio's wild sensuality. The smooth, rich milk chocolate coating then satisfies the Scorpion's desire for sweets.

Scorpions are intense, headstrong, forever mysterious, and passionate about love and food. This sign's unquenchable appetite for chocolate is symbolic of their appetite for life itself.

Scorpio Milk Chocolate Truffles with Rum Raisin Cream Filling

makes 32

24 ounces milk chocolate, finely chopped

$^1/_4$ cup heavy cream

4 teaspoons dark rum

$^1/_3$ cup finely chopped raisins

1 ounce white chocolate, finely chopped, optional

"There's no such thing as bad sex? Well for me, there's no such thing as bad chocolate." —WOODY ALLEN

1. Place 8 ounces of the milk chocolate in the top of a double boiler over simmering water. Melt, stirring frequently, until smooth. Bring the cream to a boil and pour it over the chocolate. Whisk until smooth, then whisk in the rum and raisins. Freeze for 1 hour, until stiff but still sticky.

2. Refrigerate a baking sheet and line it with wax or parchment paper. Using a melon baller, shape the chocolate into 3/4-inch balls on the baking sheet. Freeze for 2 hours.

3. Temper (see How to Temper Chocolate, page 90) the remaining milk chocolate. Using a knife to slide the balls off the paper (they will still be sticky) and a fork or candy-dipper to dip, coat the chocolates one at a time. Place on a baking sheet lined with parchment or wax paper. Let stand until set.

4. To decorate, place the white chocolate in a glass measuring cup or bowl and microwave on medium for 30 seconds. Stir, then microwave for 10 to 30 seconds longer, or until melted. Scrape the chocolate into a small plastic sandwich bag. Snip off a small piece of a bottom corner and pipe the Scorpio sign onto each truffle. Refrigerate until set.

Scorpio Chocolate Martini

makes 1

1 tablespoon sugar

1 tablespoon cocoa powder

$^1/_4$ cup chocolate syrup

$1^1/_2$ ounces plain or vanilla-flavored vodka

$2^1/_2$ ounces light crème de cacao

Crushed ice

Chocolate olives or chocolate shavings, optional

1. In a small bowl, mix together the sugar and cocoa powder. Pour the chocolate syrup onto a small plate or saucer. Dip a martini glass rim into the syrup and then into the cocoa mixture. Place in the freezer to chill.

2. In a martini shaker, combine the vodka, crème de cacao, and 3/4 shaker of crushed ice. Shake until a light frosting appears on the outside of the shaker. Strain into the chilled martini glass. Garnish with either chocolate olives (available at specialty stores) or shavings. To create shavings, use a vegetable peeler to shave strips of chocolate from a chocolate bar. Chill shavings until ready to serve. Serve immediately.

DARK CHOCOLATE MARTINI
Substitute an equal amount of dark crème de cacao for the light and follow the remaining directions.

"Rock [Hudson] and I hit it off right away and acted like a pair of kids. During our toots, we concocted the best drink I ever tasted—a chocolate martini made with vodka, Hershey syrup, and Kahlúa. How we survived, I'll never know."

—ELIZABETH TAYLOR,
Elizabeth Taylor Takes Off

Water Sign

PISCES

THE FISH
February 19–March 20

MILK CHOCOLATE—COVERED MARSHMALLOWS

Pisceans are both social and modest, and they have great intuitive powers. Marshmallow filling provides this mystical dreamer with a delicious cushion to float on, while the sweet milk chocolate represents Pisces's good-natured friendliness.

Pisceans are generous souls. When presented with a gift of chocolate, they promptly turn around and share it with friends and family.

"After eating chocolate you feel godlike, as though you can conquer enemies, lead armies, entice lovers."

—EMILY LUCHETTI,
AMERICAN PASTRY CHEF

Pisces Milk Chocolate–Covered Marshmallows

makes 16

Confectioners' sugar

1 cup granulated sugar

$^1/_2$ cup water

1 envelope ($2^1/_2$ teaspoons) unflavored gelatin

$1^1/_4$ pounds milk chocolate, tempered
(see How to Temper Chocolate, page 90)

1 ounce white chocolate, finely chopped, optional

1. Sift confectioners' sugar liberally over the bottom of an 8 × 8-inch baking pan and set aside.

2. In a small saucepan over high heat, combine the granulated sugar and half (¹/₄ cup) of the water. Bring to a boil and heat, without stirring, until the mixture reaches the soft ball stage (238°F. on a candy thermometer). If sugar crystals begin to coat the interior sides of the saucepan during boiling, lightly brush down the sides with a pastry brush dipped in cold water.

3. Meanwhile, in the bowl of an electric mixer, soften the gelatin in the remaining ¹/₄ cup of water. When the sugar has reached the proper temperature, whisk it into the gelatin and continue whisking until the gelatin and sugar are well mixed. Then, on medium-high speed, whip the mixture until stiff peaks form, about 5 to 6 minutes. With a spatula, scrape the mixture into the prepared pan and spread until evenly distributed. Let stand for 2 hours to set up.

4. Cut the marshmallow into 16 pieces and lay them on a sheet of wax paper dusted with confectioners' sugar. To dip into the tempered chocolate, shake off any excess sugar and, using a fork or candy-dipper, dip the marshmallows one at a time. Place on a baking sheet lined with parchment or wax paper and refrigerate until set.

5. To decorate the tops, place the white chocolate in a glass measuring cup or bowl and microwave on medium for 30 to 40 seconds. Stir, then microwave for 10 to 40 seconds longer, or until melted. Scrape the chocolate into a small plastic sandwich bag. Snip off a small piece of a bottom corner and pipe the Pisces sign onto each chocolate. Refrigerate until set.

Pisces Chocolate Pudding

makes 4¹/₄ cups or 4 servings

¹/₃ cup unsweetened cocoa powder

¹/₃ cup cornstarch

¹/₃ cup sugar

4 cups (1 quart) milk

1 ounce milk chocolate, finely chopped

1 teaspoon vanilla extract

Combine the cocoa, cornstarch, and sugar in a medium-size heavy saucepan. Over medium heat, slowly whisk in the milk until a smooth paste has formed. Whisk in the remainder of the milk, then bring to a boil, whisking constantly. Remove from the heat and add the chocolate. Stir until the chocolate has dissolved. Stir in the vanilla and pour into 4 individual serving cups to cool. Serve chilled.

"Chocolate has a very interesting melting point. It is above the temperature of the hands but below that of the mouth. Which means it will melt in your mouth but not in your hands. It will also take the heat out of your mouth and so make it feel quite cool, which is very pleasant."

—Dr. Peter Barham, physicist,
Bristol University, Scotland

Gemini, Libra, and Aquarius

THEIR BIRTH CHOCOLATE: WHITE CHOCOLATE

White chocolate consists of cocoa butter, fats, sugar, and milk, a subtle, airy combination that intrigues the air signs.

Gemini, Libra, and Aquarius are clever, intellectual people pleasers. The subtle flavor of white chocolate appeals to their discerning taste buds and their love of elegance.

A Gemini is characterized by intelligent conversation, spontaneous decisions, and a dislike of difficult choices. Then again, maybe the Twin doesn't necessarily have to make choices in order to progress.

The justice-loving sign of Libra is most comfortable when all is balanced and equal, and may spend so much time trying to make a fair decision that the problem may solve itself first.

Free-spirited and open-minded, an Aquarius doesn't like to be fenced in. Instead, this independent thinker prefers to know that all doors are open.

Air Sign

GEMINI

THE TWINS
May 21– June 21

THE PERFECT CHOCOLATE FOR A GEMINI:
WHITE CHOCOLATE TRUFFLES
WITH GREEN TEA GANACHE

Symbolized by the Twins, Geminis are versatile souls whose own opinions are often in conflict.

They are social butterflies, flitting from place to place, and it can be difficult to get a Gemini to make a solid decision. White chocolate truffles filled with green tea ganache are the ideal indulgence for this easily swayed sign because there is no need to choose between yin and yang!

Gemini White Chocolate Truffles with Green Tea Ganache

makes 35 to 40

$^1/_3$ cup heavy cream

3 green tea bags

24 ounces white chocolate, finely chopped

1 ounce dark chocolate, finely chopped, optional

"Henry Green was a boy who loved chocolate. He liked it
bitter, sweet, dark, light, and daily; for breakfast, lunch,
dinner, and snacks; in cakes, candy bars, milk, and in every
other conceivable form. Henry probably loved chocolate
more than any boy in the history of the world."
—Robert K. Smith, *Chocolate Fever*, 1972

1. Bring the cream to a boil in a small saucepan and place the tea bags in it. Cover and let steep for 5 minutes. Gently squeeze excess cream from the bags back into the remaining cream and discard the bags.

2. Meanwhile, place 8 ounces of the white chocolate in a bowl over simmering water. Melt, stirring occasionally, until smooth. Bring the cream to a boil again and whisk it into the melted chocolate until smooth. Refrigerate until thick and stiff, about 3 to 4 hours.

3. Chill a baking sheet and line it with wax or parchment paper. Use a melon baller or spoon to shape the chocolate into 3/4-inch balls on the baking sheet (this mixture is very sticky). Cover with plastic wrap and freeze until chilled, about 1 to 2 hours.

4. Temper (see How to Temper Chocolate, page 90) the remaining white chocolate and, using a fork or candy-dipper, dip the chocolates one at a time. Place on a baking sheet lined with parchment or wax paper and refrigerate until set.

5. To decorate, place the dark chocolate in a glass measuring cup or bowl and microwave on medium for 30 seconds. Stir, then microwave for 10 to 30 seconds longer, or until melted. Scrape the chocolate into a small plastic sandwich bag. Snip off a small piece of a bottom corner and pipe the Gemini sign onto each truffle. Refrigerate until set.

Gemini Black-and-White Cookies

makes 18

COOKIES

2 cups sifted all-purpose flour

$^1/_2$ teaspoon baking soda

$^1/_4$ teaspoon salt

2 ounces white chocolate, finely chopped

$^1/_2$ cup (1 stick) unsalted butter

$^3/_4$ cup granulated sugar

1 large egg, at room temperature

1 teaspoon vanilla extract

$^1/_2$ cup milk

DARK AND WHITE CHOCOLATE ICINGS

$^1/_3$ cup plus $^1/_4$ cup heavy cream

2 ounces bittersweet chocolate, finely chopped

3 ounces white chocolate, finely chopped

2 tablespoons confectioners' sugar

1. Preheat the oven to 375°F. Line three cookie sheets with parchment paper, or grease and flour them.

2. Sift together the flour, baking soda, and salt and set aside.

3. In a double boiler over simmering water, melt the white chocolate, stirring frequently until smooth. Stir in the butter and granulated sugar and continue stirring until the butter is melted. Remove from the heat, add the egg and vanilla, and stir until smooth. Add in half the dry ingredients, then all of the milk. Stir in the remaining dry ingredients and continue stirring until smooth.

4. Using a heaping tablespoonful, spoon the dough onto the prepared sheets, keeping the cookies 2 to 3 inches apart. Bake two sheets at a time, for 12 to 15 minutes, or until the cookies spring back when lightly touched with a fingertip. Let the cookies cool for 5 minutes, then transfer them to a rack to completely cool.

5. To prepare the dark chocolate icing, bring 1/3 cup of the cream to a boil in a small saucepan over high heat. Off the heat, throw in the chopped bittersweet chocolate and stir until very smooth. Let cool until room temperature and the icing is thickened and spreadable. To make the white chocolate icing, bring the remaining 1/4 cup cream to a boil. Add the white chocolate and stir until smooth. Sift in the confectioners' sugar and let cool to room temperature. To decorate the cookies, using a small spatula, spread half of the top of each cookie with the dark chocolate icing, then spread the remaining half with the white chocolate. Let stand until set.

LIBRA

THE SCALES
September 23–October 22

WHITE AND DARK CHOCOLATE LAYER CANDIES

A candy that combines white and dark chocolate provides balance and satisfies Libra's desire to find harmony in all things.

A dispenser of justice and lover of romance, Libra weighs all the issues on a personal scale. True Libras make decisions based on the careful analysis of facts. Always balancing opposite points of view, they know precisely how to have their chocolate and eat it, too.

Libra White and Dark Chocolate Layer Candies

makes about 20

1¹/₄ pounds bittersweet or semisweet chocolate, tempered
(see How to Temper Chocolate, page 90)

10 ounces white chocolate, tempered

1 ounce white chocolate, finely chopped, optional

"It was not a human voice; yet it had a quality—a timbre, even
in the monotone with which it spoke—that made me think of
Chocolate as a 'he.'"

—David Alexander, *The Chocolate Spy*, 1978

1. With a pastry bag fitted with a 1-inch plain tip, pipe the dark chocolate into the candy molds (which can be purchased from candy and confectionery manufacture suppliers or other specialty stores). Drop each mold (open side up) gently onto the work surface to force out any bubbles. After 2 minutes, turn the mold upside down and shake out any excess chocolate onto a piece of wax paper, using a circular motion to coat the mold completely. With a knife or offset spatula, scrape across the top of the mold to remove any excess chocolate. Place the molds face down, so they thicken at their bases. Refrigerate for 10 to 20 minutes, or until firm. Remove any excess chocolate on the wax paper and retemper.

2. Pipe the white chocolate into the molds, almost to the top. Drop each mold gently again (open side up) to level the chocolate.

3. Pipe in more tempered dark chocolate to cover the white chocolate. Scrape the top with a knife or offset spatula to level the chocolates, then refrigerate until set, about 10 to 20 minutes. Invert the molds onto a sheet of wax paper.

4. To decorate the tops, place the chopped white chocolate in a glass measuring cup or bowl and microwave on medium for 30 to 40 seconds. Stir, then microwave for 10 to 40 seconds longer, or until melted. Scrape the chocolate into a small plastic sandwich bag. Snip off a small piece of a bottom corner and pipe the Libra sign onto each chocolate. Refrigerate until set.

Libra White Chocolate Cake

serves 8

CAKE

3 ounces white chocolate, finely chopped

$^1/_2$ cup ($2^1/_2$ ounces) whole almonds

8 tablespoons ($^1/_2$ cup) sugar

1 cup all-purpose flour

$^1/_2$ teaspoon baking powder

$^1/_4$ teaspoon salt

$^1/_4$ cup ($^1/_2$ stick) unsalted butter, softened

2 large eggs, at room temperature

$^1/_4$ teaspoon vanilla extract

$^1/_4$ teaspoon almond extract

2 tablespoons milk

GLAZE

6 ounces white chocolate, finely chopped

$^1/_3$ cup heavy cream

1 ounce bittersweet chocolate, finely chopped, optional

1. Preheat the oven to 325°F. Grease a 9-inch round cake pan and line the base of the pan with parchment or wax paper. Flour the sides and tap out any excess.

2. Melt the white chocolate in the top of a double boiler set over simmering water. Set aside to cool.

3. In the bowl of a food processor fitted with a steel blade, grind the almonds with 2 tablespoons of the sugar until very fine. Transfer the nuts to a bowl and add the flour, baking powder, and salt. Mix well.

4. In the bowl of an electric mixer, beat the butter and remaining 6 tablespoons of the sugar until fluffy, about 3 minutes. Add the eggs, one at a time, beating well after each addition. Beat in the cooled chocolate. Beat in the vanilla and almond extracts.

5. With the mixer on low, alternately add the flour mixture and the milk to the butter mixture. Beat only until blended. Turn the batter into the prepared pan and spread evenly. Bake for about 35 minutes, or until a cake tester inserted in the middle of the cake comes out clean. Cool for 10 minutes, then run a thin-bladed knife around the edge and turn out onto a rack. Let the cake cool completely.

6. To make the glaze, place the white chocolate in a bowl. Bring the cream to a boil and pour it over the chocolate. Whisk until smooth. Place the cake on its rack over a sheet of wax paper. Pour the glaze over the cake, using a spatula or knife to push the glaze over the sides. Refrigerate until the glaze has set.

7. To decorate, melt the bittersweet chocolate in the microwave on high power for 1 minute, or in the top of a double boiler set over simmering water. Whisk until smooth. Scrape the melted chocolate into a small plastic sandwich bag and cut off a small piece of a bottom corner. Over a sheet of wax paper, squeeze the chocolate back and forth, making thin lines. Place the wax paper on a baking sheet and refrigerate until set. Peel off the chocolate lines and place them on top of the cake. Serve at room temperature or lightly chilled.

AQUARIUS

THE WATER BEARER
January 20–February 18

THE PERFECT CHOCOLATE FOR AN AQUARIUS:
WHITE CHOCOLATE MINTS

The surprise-loving Aquarius enjoys the burst of refreshing mint flavor hidden beneath the sweet white chocolate covering.

Aquarius, the Water Bearer, is spontaneous, popular, eccentric, and independent. Aquarians would be happy if everyone in the universe had a chocolate mint on his or her pillow.

Aquarius White Chocolate Mints

makes about 25

Confectioners' sugar

1 teaspoon pure mint extract

Basic Fondant Filling (see page 92)

1¹/₄ pounds white chocolate, tempered
(see How to Temper Chocolate, page 90)

1 ounce bittersweet or semisweet chocolate,
finely chopped, optional

"Venice is like eating an entire box of chocolate." —TRUMAN CAPOTE

1. On a work surface liberally dusted with confectioners' sugar, knead the mint extract into the fondant until evenly distributed. Roll into a 3/4-inch cylinder and cut into 1/2-inch pieces. Flatten each piece into a 1 1/2 × 1-inch oval disk with the palm of your hand and place them on a wax paper–lined sheet. Chill for 15 minutes.

2. With a fork or candy-dipper, dip each piece of fondant into the white chocolate. Place on a cookie sheet lined with parchment or wax paper. Refrigerate until the chocolate is firm.

3. Place the bittersweet chocolate in a glass measuring cup or bowl and microwave on medium for 30 seconds. Stir, then microwave for 10 to 30 seconds longer, or until melted. Scrape the chocolate into a small plastic sandwich bag. Snip off a small piece of a bottom corner and pipe the Aquarius sign on each candy. Refrigerate until set.

Aquarian Brownies

makes 16

8 ounces (2 sticks) unsalted butter

4 ounces unsweetened chocolate, coarsely chopped

2 tablespoons espresso coffee powder

2 cups dark brown sugar, lightly packed

4 large eggs

2 tablespoons dark rum

1 cup all-purpose flour

$^1/_4$ teaspoon salt

$^1/_2$ cup chopped pecans

6 ounces white chocolate, coarsely chopped (about 1 cup)

1. Preheat the oven to 375°F. Line an 8 × 8 × 2-inch baking pan with aluminum foil, letting the foil overhang the sides. Grease the foil.

2. In the top of a double boiler set over simmering water, combine the butter, unsweetened chocolate, and espresso powder. Stir frequently until melted and smooth. Remove from the heat and stir in the brown sugar until smooth. Then, using a spatula or wooden spoon, beat in the eggs, one at a time, beating well after each addition. Beat in the rum, then the flour and salt. Fold in the pecans and white chocolate, just until evenly distributed. Pour into the prepared pan.

3. Bake the brownies just until they pull away from the sides of the pan, about 40 to 45 minutes. Remove to a rack and let cool completely. To serve, use the foil to lift the brownies out and cut into 16 squares.

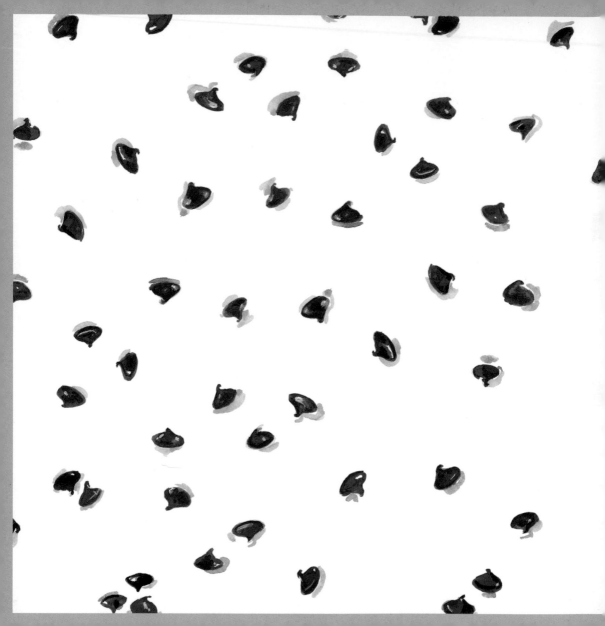

CHOCOLATE
BASICS

How to Temper Chocolate

$1^1/_4$ pounds bittersweet,
semisweet, white, or milk chocolate

candy thermometer

STOVETOP DIRECTIONS

Finely chop 1 pound of the chocolate. Leave the remaining 1/4 pound in large pieces. Melt the chopped chocolate in the top of a double boiler set over simmering water, stirring occasionally until smooth, shiny, and melted. Remove the top of the double boiler from the heat and stir in the remaining 1/4 pound of chocolate. Cool the chocolate by stirring until it reaches 90°F. for bittersweet or semisweet chocolate or 88°F. for white or milk chocolate. Remove any remaining chunks of unmelted chocolate (reserve for the next time). The chocolate is now in temper and can be piped or used for dipping. To maintain an even heat for dipping, set the container with the tempered chocolate in a bowl filled with 1/2 inch of warm water.

MICROWAVE DIRECTIONS

Finely chop 1 pound of the chocolate. Leave the remaining 1/4 pound in large pieces. Melt the chopped chocolate in a large glass measuring cup or mixing bowl on high power (for bittersweet or semisweet chocolate) or low power (for white and milk chocolates) for 1 minute. Stir well and microwave in 30-second increments (stirring after each), until the chocolate is melted and smooth. If the bittersweet or semisweet chocolate is above 90°F. when melted, add the reserved chunks and stir to cool it to 90°F. If white or milk chocolate is above 88°F., add the chunks as above to cool down. When the desired temperature has been reached, remove and set aside any large chunks. The chocolate is now in temper and can be piped or used for dipping. To maintain an even heat for dipping, set the container with the tempered chocolate in a bowl filled with 1/2 inch of warm water.

Basic Fondant

makes about 3/4 pound

$^1/_4$ cup water

$^1/_4$ cup heavy cream

$1^1/_2$ cups sugar

$1^1/_2$ teapoons light corn syrup

1. Bring the water and cream to a boil in a large heavy-bottomed saucepan. Stir in the sugar and corn syrup until dissolved. Bring to a boil and cook without stirring, until the mixture reaches 238°F., or the soft ball stage. Sprinkle a cold surface (a marble slab or baking sheet) with water and pour the syrup onto the surface, without scraping out the bottom of the pan. Cool to lukewarm (about 110°F.).

2. Using a spatula or a clean putty knife, work the syrup by lifting and folding until it becomes white and creamy. Transfer it to a surface dusted with confectioners' sugar and knead the fondant until smooth and creamy. Shape it into a ball and cover it with a damp cloth. Place the fondant in a zippered plastic bag and refrigerate overnight to ripen.

ACKNOWLEDGMENTS

This book is in honor of my mother, whose chocolate desserts always gave me inspiration; my grandmother, who taught my mother the art of Hungarian baking; my father, who introduced us to French pastry; my brothers, who bought me bakery cookies; my sons, Sidney and Peter, who played my game of chocolate hide-and-seek and understand my difficulties in sharing chocolate; Giuliana, who joined us bringing chocolates; and to our newest addition, Elias Cash.

Special thanks to my editors, Annetta Hanna for her artistic vision and Liz Royles for her graceful editing; my agent, Claire Booss, whose contribution to this book went far beyond agenting;

astrologer Claire Guris for her words and wisdom; Susie Schwartz, whose early insights were so helpful; Margaret Kaplan for her support and encouragement; Jean Galton for all recipes with the exception of Alice Nagy for Capricorn and Leo cake recipes, Marshal Nagy for his Aries cake, and Sid Reitzfeld for the chocolate martini.

Thanks to my friends who plied me with boxes of chocolate; your generosity has always exceeded mine. I am forever grateful.

Chocolate Astrology is the result of time spent painting, eating chocolate, and stargazing. This book is in memory of Gusta Friedman and Roy Lee.